Remembering the Rocket

Remembering the Rocket

A CELEBRATION

CRAIG MacINNIS, EDITOR

A PETER GODDARD BOOK

Published in 1998 by Stoddart Publishing Co. Limited
34 Lesmill Road, Toronto, Canada M3B 2T6
180 Varick Street, 9th Floor, New York, New York 10014

Distributed in Canada by:
General Distribution Services Ltd.
325 Humber College Blvd., Toronto, Ontario M9W 7C3
Tel. (416) 213-1919   Fax (416) 213-1917
Email customer.service@ccmailgw.genpub.com

Distributed in the United States by:
General Distribution Services Inc.
85 River Rock Drive, Suite 202, Buffalo, New York 14207
Toll-free Tel. 1-800-805-1083   Toll-free Fax 1-800-481-6207
Email gdsinc@genpub.com

02   01   00   99   98   1   2   3   4   5

Canadian Cataloguing in Publication Data

Remembering the Rocket: a celebration

"A PETER GODDARD BOOK"   ISBN 0-7737-3128-8

1. Richard, Maurice, 1921–   . 2. Hockey players — Quebec (Province) — Biography. I. MacInnis, Craig.

GV848.5.R5R45 1998   796.962'092   C98-931479-0
Printed and bound in Canada

ART DIRECTION AND DESIGN: BILL DOUGLAS @ THE BANG

RESEARCHER: LIZA HERZ

Page 128 constitutes a continuation of this copyright page.

TABLE OF CONTENTS

DURING HIS 18-YEAR CAREER WITH THE MONTREAL
CANADIENS, MAURICE RICHARD NEVER MADE
MORE THAN $50,000 IN A SINGLE SEASON,
INCLUDING BONUS MONEY. IN AN AGE WHEN THE
AVERAGE NHLER MAKES MORE THAN A MILLION
DOLLARS A YEAR, RICHARD'S SLENDER PAYPACKET
SEEMS ALMOST POIGNANT, A THROWBACK TO THE
DAYS BEFORE HOCKEY BECAME SYNONYMOUS WITH
BIG BUSINESS.

IN THE MODERN NHL — WITH ITS RAPID
EXPANSION TO THE SOUTHERN U.S., ITS USURIOUS
"LICENSING FEES" FOR SEASON TICKETHOLDERS,
ITS RIDICULOUS SEPTEMBER TO JUNE PLAYING
SCHEDULE — HOCKEY'S CORE VALUES SEEM IN
SAD RETREAT.

MAYBE THAT'S WHY THE ROCKET SUDDENLY
SEEMS SO RELEVANT AGAIN. AS A PLAYER, HE
STOOD FOR THE VERY THINGS — PRIDE,

DEDICATION, ÉLAN — THAT MANY FIND MISSING FROM THE MODERN GAME. AT THE END OF THE 1997–98 SEASON, LEAGUE COMMISSIONER GARY BETTMAN ANNOUNCED THAT THE NHL'S GOAL-SCORING LEADER WOULD HENCEFORTH RECEIVE THE MAURICE RICHARD TROPHY, AN OVERDUE NOD TO HOCKEY'S GREATEST NATURAL MARKSMAN. NINETEEN-NINETY-EIGHT ALSO SAW RICHARD INDUCTED INTO THE ORDER OF CANADA, CONFIRMING THAT HIS ON-ICE FEATS TRANSCENDED MERE SPORT.

IN THIS COLLECTION OF VINTAGE NEWSPAPER AND MAGAZINE ARTICLES, ROCKET'S LIFE AND TIMES ARE CONJURED IN VIVID PROSE, FROM AN ACCOUNT OF THE INFAMOUS MONTREAL RIOT OF 1955, TO STORIES ANALYZING HIS ON-ICE GREATNESS, TO A TOUCHING PROFILE OF RICHARD THE FAMILY MAN.

Rocket
Redux

FOR MANY OF US BORN TOO LATE TO RECALL HIS BLUELINE-TO-GOALMOUTH INTENSITY, THE PHENOME-NON OF MAURICE RICHARD DIDN'T FULLY REGISTER UNTIL 36 YEARS AFTER HE HAD QUIT THE GAME.

The occasion was the opening of the $230-million Molson Centre in March of 1996, when the Montreal Canadiens unfurled the commemorative banners of players whose numbers they had retired.

It was a heady roster: Howie Morenz, Jacques Plante, Doug Harvey, Jean Beliveau, Guy Lafleur and Richard's younger brother, Henri. Beliveau,

1

the Pocket Rocket and especially Lafleur are mod-
ern-era gods, their careers framed by ubiquitous
television cameras and Danny Gallivan's keening
play-by-play commentary. If anyone typified the

fire-wagon mythologies of Les Habitants for fans
of the recent past, it would be Lafleur, the Canadiens' last great exemplar of end-to-end artistry.

But in the pre-game ceremony that March
night, the ovation for Rocket Richard — a player
whose greatest on-ice achievements arguably pre-
ceded the television era — went well beyond

INTO THE FUTURE: RICHARD LEADS
HABS OUT OF THE FORUM AND INTO
THE NEW MOLSON CENTRE.

2

ordinary fandom. The hubbub had actually started several nights earlier, when Richard had led a
cavalcade of new and old Canadiens out of their
long-time St. Catherine Street residence, the
Montreal Forum.

It was hard to say which experience was
more charged: Richard bidding adieu to the Habs'
storied past, or Richard leading the franchise into
its high-tech future.

The applause that greeted him at the Molson
Centre was a 10-minute-long crescendo of pure
unadulterated feeling.

It sounded like the collective exhalation of a
ghost nation, a long-dormant version of ourselves
(pre-Trudeaumania, pre-Bettman NHL), brought
back by a man who had symbolized, and given
shape to, the whole damn thing.

In the stands, Prime Minister Jean Chrétien
and Quebec premier Lucien Bouchard, political
adversaries representing two visions of Quebec
and Canada, seemed comically dwarfed by the
fanfare.

Like everyone else, Chrétien and Bouchard

were reduced to spectators, unable to manufacture political opportunity from a moment which 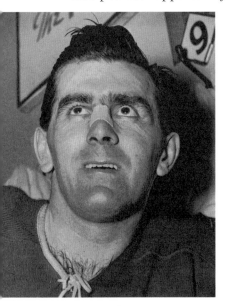 engendered a kind of unity that no piece of legislation or act of public office could hope to match.

Richard, for his part, seemed on the verge of tears, shaking his head and occasionally swiping the air with his hand, as if to subdue the crowd's emotions.

Of all the sporting moments to have cut across the country's social and political lines — Paul Henderson's 1972 game-winner for Team Canada, Joe Carter's bottom-of-the-ninth homer against Philadelphia to win the 1993 World Series for the Toronto Blue Jays — the Molson Centre dedication seems, to me, the most profound.

It says that we haven't forgotten who we are, or where we came from. Even in a media-saturated age where memory is quickly dimmed by newer and bigger stars (Wayne Gretzky, Mario Lemieux, Eric Lindros), Richard's legend continues to shine.

If he was a totem of French-Canadian aspirations in the era of Duplessis, he was, for English-speaking Canadians, a benchmark against which we measured our own place in the firmament. I grew up in St. Catharines, Ontario, and was only four years old when Richard announced his retirement from hockey in the fall of 1960. Though I never saw him play, he shaped my hockey consciousness — even my sense of the country.

This was largely due to my father, who would not hesitate to offer endless variations on what had been the defining quandary of post-war hockey debates, a.k.a. the

"Howe–Richard thing."

Detroit's Gordie Howe, the era's other famous No. 9, was, in every way, the perfect foil to Richard. English rather than French. Methodical rather than temperamental. A slick playmaker rather than a coal-eyed force of nature. Implicit in those differences, at least to a kid from St. Catharines, were the differences between English- and French-speaking Canada. From Howe and Richard, I gleaned a sense of the country's weird emotional breadth. From their contradictory styles, a sense that there was more than one way to get from Point A to Point B.

Howe, for me, equalled cool efficiency and the deceptively languorous stride. Richard, on the other hand, represented blazing passion and full-bore intensity, a willingness to risk injury — and to inflict it — in a headlong determination to score. For Howe, hockey was a

TOP: GORDIE HOWE, RICHARD'S NEMESIS. BOTTOM: THE ROCKET GETS A HEADLOCK FROM TEAMMATES.

ALTHOUGH TV WAS STILL IN ITS INFANCY IN THE 1950S, RICHARD, PERHAPS MORE THAN ANY PLAYER SINCE, SEEMS TO HAVE BEEN READY-MADE FOR THE TUBE.

game of patterns and circles; for Richard, it was a direct line to the opposition's net.

Although TV was still in its infancy in the 1950s, Richard, perhaps more than any player since, seems to have been ready-made for the tube, with its tendency to aggrandize those who perform on a heroic scale.

Writing in 1958, Toronto *Globe and Mail* columnist Jim Coleman offered an early critique on Howe's and Richard's relative value as TV icons.

"To be truthful," Coleman wrote, "the most recent converts to hockey know little of the niceties of the game. Twenty-five percent of them don't realize the puck is in the net until the goal judge turns on the red light. The work of Howe, a perfectionist, often is lost on these new spectators. However, even a casual television fan can appreciate Richard, whose every appearance includes the violent promise of thunder and lightning."

That is undoubtedly true, but I imagine there was also something that those early television broadcasts missed in their coverage of Richard. That would be his inclination toward furtiveness and introspection.

Richard's dark temperament, and his brooding looks, seem more a product of the old print traditions, of men in snap-brim fedoras with sharp tongues and tight deadlines, working the beat in shadowy corridors and sweaty dressing rooms. That's why any look back at Richard's amazing career, from his season of 50 goals in 50 games, to the infamous 1955 riot following his suspension by NHL president Clarence Campbell, is a story best told via the clippings and flash-photos of the era.

For more than anything else, Richard was a talent best summarized by the blunt, quotidien poetry of the working press, the men and women who laboured to describe and understand the enormity of his meaning, both inside and outside the hockey rink.

The journalism that captured Richard also captured the age in which his legend grew. Before

RICHARD'S DARK TEMPERAMENT, AND HIS BROODING LOOKS, SEEM MORE A PRODUCT OF THE OLD PRINT TRADITIONS, OF MEN IN SNAPBRIM FEDORAS WITH SHARP TONGUES AND TIGHT DEADLINES, WORKING THE BEAT IN SHADOWY CORRIDORS AND SWEATY DRESSING ROOMS.

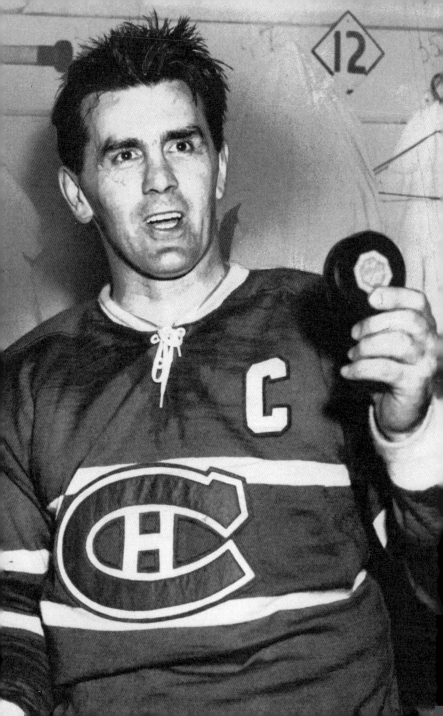

television, the print media pretty much had the whole game to themselves, and they not only reported the news but found ways to make us all think we were right there, behind the net.

Consider this dispatch from the Montreal *Gazette* during Richard's first full week in the NHL, in November of 1942: "Richard picked up the puck near his own goalmouth, broke fast and came up the centre of the ice under a full head of steam, swerved around the Rangers' defence and coasted in on Steve Buzinski. His backhand shot lodged in the upper corner of the net, completely fooling the goalie. It was an end-to-end effort reminiscent of the feats of Howie Morenz, and the full house accorded the youngster a roar of acclaim that lasted for minutes."

Writing like that I'll take any day over video replays.

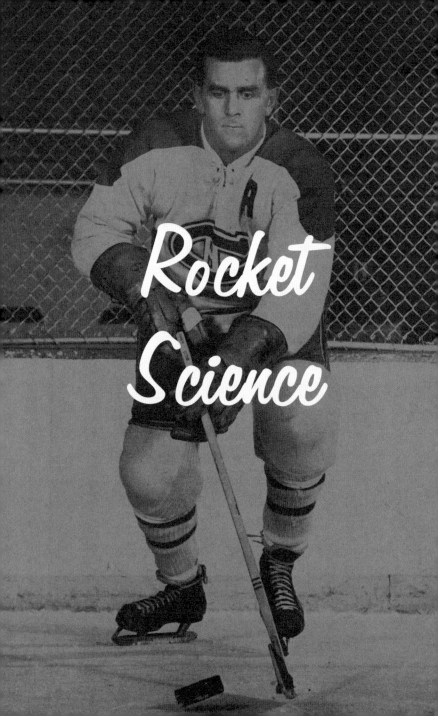

ANY MOMENT NOW MAURICE RICHARD WILL SCORE THE THREE HUNDREDTH GOAL OF HIS NATIONAL HOCKEY LEAGUE CAREER

and sometime early next spring he will break Nels Stewart's all-time record of 323 goals and thus become the greatest goal scorer in professional hockey history. There is a reasonable likelihood that Richard will score one or both of these goals while he is lying flat on his back, with at least one non-Canadien hockey player clutching his stick, another hacking at his ankles with a pair of skates and a third plucking thoughtfully at his sweater.

No hockey player living has been so put upon as Richard by the recent revolution in hockey's cultural standards — a liberalizing process which encourages the referees to ignore all but the most flagrant violations of the written rules and, in turn, encourages poor or indifferent players to cut good or great players down to size by slamming them bodily into the sides of the rinks, massaging their ribs with fibre-padded elbows, inserting the crooked blades of hockey sticks between their legs or under their armpits and generally impeding what used to be considered their lawful progress.

In consequence, modern hockey has produced many teams which stand out above their rivals but few individual players who stand out above the other individuals. For almost a decade Richard has towered over them all, both as a goal scorer and as a piece of property.

Hockey experts have never been able to explain precisely why Richard — who in action frequently looks uninspired and almost awkward — keeps on scoring so many goals. During the

ROCKET RICHARD

ELMER LACH

TOE BLAKE

THE PUNCH LINE

WHEN HE GETS WOUND UP
ON MONTREAL ICE, WITH
THE FORUM CROWDS
SHRIEKING WILDLY EACH
TIME HE GETS THE PUCK,
HE BECOMES A WHIRLING
DASHING MAN POSSESSED.

war a number of coaches, notably Frank Boucher of the New York Rangers, insisted it was because of inferior opposition but in the last two years, when competition again had reached a peak, Richard scored 85 goals and Boucher now says that Richard is the most spectacular hockey player he has ever seen. "That includes," adds Boucher with some reverence, "the greatest I'd ever seen before him, Howie Morenz."

Curiously, the determined Richard has seldom exploded in Toronto and it has taken many a long year to convince that city's hockey populace — and, with it, the national audience that views the Maple Leafs and their opponents through Foster Hewitt's Saturday night nuances — that Richard is anything more than an obscure No. 9 patrolling right wing for the Canadiens. The year Richard scored 50 goals he collected only four of them in seven games in Toronto and there have been scores of games over the years when he has had not even four shots on the net.

Richard is at his best at home. When he gets wound up on Montreal ice, with the Forum

TOP: CANADIENS' TEAM PHOTO.
BOTTOM: THE ROCKET AND LINE-
MATE ELMER LACH HUG THE CUP.

crowds shrieking wildly each time he gets the puck, he becomes a whirling dashing man possessed.

One night he arrived at the dressing room an hour before game time and informed coach Dick Irvin he was pooped. "Pooped?" enquired Irvin. "How do you mean pooped?" "Moved today," replied Richard, whose English is tinged with Jean-Baptiste. "Carried furniture up and down stairs all afternoon. Feel pooped."

This came about three days after Christmas in 1944 and Richard had bought a new home for his family. The Canadiens were playing Detroit that night, always a rugged opponent at the Forum, and the pooped Richard moved lethargically onto the ice. Before the night was out the fizzled Rocket was sizzling; he scored five goals, got three assists as Canadiens won 9–1.

Richard seldom makes headlines off the ice, but his attack on referee Hugh McLean in the lobby of New York's Piccadilly Hotel was one of the [1950–51] season's most wildly debated episodes. He did this twelve hours after a game in

Montreal in which he'd swung on Detroit's Leo Reise who had jeered at him for getting a penalty. "A man can take just so much. I was skating close to the Detroit net when Sid Abel grabbed me by the chin, nearly twisted my head off and spun me right around. I drew the referee's attention to this . . . but he laughed in my face. As I skated away I said: 'This is the damnedest thing yet.' And then McLean rushed up and put me off." As he skated toward the penalty box Reise snickered at him and Richard swung at the Detroit defenceman and drew an additional misconduct penalty from McLean. The following morning, as the Canadiens arrived in New York from Montreal for a Sunday night game with the Rangers, Richard encountered McLean and linesman Jim Primeau in the hotel lobby. He grabbed McLean by the collar and tried to punch him but was restrained by Primeau, who began throwing punches at Richard.

Out of all this, a week after the incident, the Rocket was fined $500 by NHL president Clarence Campbell, who declined to suspend the player (as he had done in similar cases involving

"IF I SUSPENDED RICHARD, A GREAT DRAWING CARD WHEREVER HE GOES, IT WOULD AFFECT THE ATTENDANCE OF THE LEAGUE."

other players) on the fairly implausible grounds that "the suspension of a great hockey star is not justified if it reflects in the gate receipts," to quote Bob Hesketch of the Toronto *Telegram* who interviewed Campbell after the fine was announced. "We're trying to conduct a business," Campbell continued. "If I suspended Richard, a great drawing card wherever he goes, it would affect the attendance of the league."

Two years ago, while the Toronto Maple Leafs were having trouble holding fourth place, their president, Conn Smythe, sent instructions to his coach, Hap Day, that he was to present a blank cheque to [Canadiens' general manager] Selke to be filled in with any amount up to $135,000 in exchange for Richard. Smythe was "grandstanding," according to Selke, who says Richard is the sort of competitor that money cannot buy.

Though Richard is not a big man physically, Wally Stanowski, defenceman for the New York Rangers, says he is the hardest man in the league to stop because of his strength. "I've had him completely covered," Stanowski claims, "and he'll make a pass at the blueline. Somehow he'll still manage to cut in on the net, often carrying me on his back, and get his shot away." Turk Broda, Toronto goalkeeper for fifteen seasons, says Richard's shot is the most difficult to stop, not because of its velocity but because of its

uncanny accuracy from any angle. "He'll be standing in front of the net, maybe 20 feet out, waiting for a pass out," says Broda. "He'll have his back to the goal and he'll be surrounded by

A GLASS ACT: RICHARD SHATTERS
NEWLY INSTALLED PROTECTIVE
GLASS AT MAPLE LEAF GARDENS.

our players. But if the puck comes out he some-how can whirl and swipe at it, backhand or the other way, and drive it dead for a corner. I think half the time he doesn't know where it's going himself, yet invariably it will just skim the post and deflect into the net."

Strong and durable, the Rocket almost didn't get to the starting gate. Born in Montreal, August 4, 1921, he very nearly didn't become an NHL player at all because he showed signs of being brittle — bumps and spills frequently produced fractures.

He first attracted attention as a scoring star with the Verdun Juniors in the 1939–40 season and as a 19-year-old rightwinger he joined the Montreal Canadiens of the Quebec Senior Hockey League. In the first game of the season, against the Quebec Aces, he was tripped and sent crashing into the boards. He broke his left ankle.

"I play aroun' 20 games the next year," he recalls, "still with the Canadiens seniors and then I fall against the net. This time the left arm is broke."

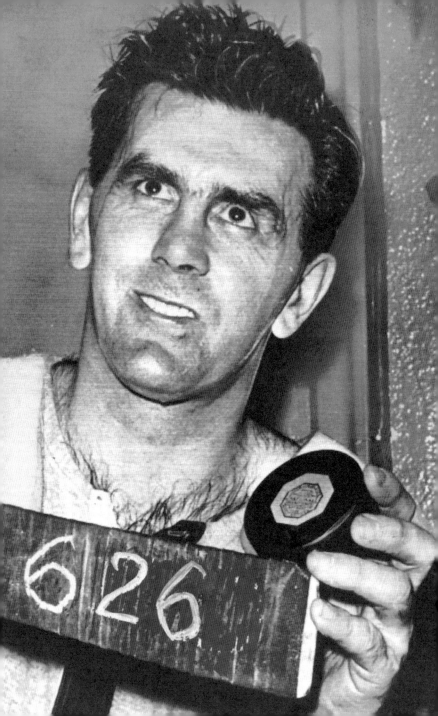

He got back in time for the playoffs and scored six goals while his team was being eliminated by Ottawa in a four-game semifinal. The NHL Canadiens signed him on the strength of his playoff performance. Teamed as a rookie with Gordie Drillon and Buddy O'Connor he scored five goals and got six assists in 16 games; then he broke his right ankle and once again was out for the season.

Early the following year, the 1943–44 season, it looked like the same story. After a couple of games he twisted his shoulder and was lost for two weeks. But then he was placed beside Elmer Lach and Toe Blake on what became known as the Punch Line and scored 32 goals in collecting 54 scoring points. The next year he produced 50 goals and became the most colourful player in professional hockey. As Ted Reeve of the Toronto *Telegram* once observed: "If I had to pay to get in, it'd be worth the price of admission to see him."

RICHARD POSES WITH MILESTONE PUCK, REPRESENTING TOTAL REGULAR SEASON AND PLAYOFF GOALS.

"I MET MAURICE WHEN I WAS 13. MY OLDER BROTHER WAS PLAYING HOCKEY AND HE USED TO RAVE ABOUT MAURICE RICHARD.

Maurice was scoring four or five goals every game. Then he brought him home to meet us. Maurice was 17 then, so shy, so quiet. Remember, mama?"

Mrs. Norchet: "I remember. His clothes were so, I shouldn't say, but not right. Not poor, but just . . . you know. My heart went out to him. He used to comb his hair straight back, very long. One day I took a comb and parted it on the side and combed it for him. 'There,' I told him. 'That's better.' He still parts it that way."

Lucille: "Maurice had no girl, but he always came to our house after the hockey games with all the

rest. We would roll up the rugs and dance and eat peanuts and potato chips and drink soft drinks. Teenagers don't have a good time like that any more, do they? I wonder why. I was very young but I taught Maurice to dance. After a while, he was very good at the rumba. He liked it . . .

"Except for hockey, he didn't have friends. He was so shy, so quiet. He just watched people. Maurice had it tough when he was young, really tough." (Richard's father was a CPR machinist, out of work for a two-year period during the depression. Maurice was the oldest of eight children.)

Mrs. Norchet: "You should have seen her leave for the church. Most brides are nervous, but Lucille was as gay as a bird, turned and waved like she was going to a movie. Me, I was crying . . .

"Maurice waits at the hospital when Lucille is having a baby. It doesn't matter how long it takes, he won't leave. Would you believe it, he cries. My sons never shed a tear when their wives are having babies, but Maurice weeps every time."

THE ROCKET PRESENTS A PRIZE TO YOUNG TONY PEARSON AT SIMPSON'S COWBOY CORAL IN 1951.

Lucille: "He's supposed to be so hard, but wait till you see him at home. He's so gentle and kind, so good to the kids. Too good, I tell him."

Mrs. Norchet: "Remember [Lucille's oldest daughter] Hugette's ski pants?"

Lucille [laughing]: "She wanted the stretchy kind,

they cost $40. Maurice got mad and said it was crazy for a girl to have ski pants that cost $40. The next day he went and bought them himself."

Mrs. Norchet: "And when they're sick he almost drives Lucille crazy. He keeps asking her if they have had their medicine, if it is the right kind, does the doctor know about it. Same when she isn't well. If she forgets to take her medicine, he is wild!"

Lucille: "We used to fight a lot when we were first married but not any more. He is much happier now, much more contented. He is living a good life and it makes him feel, well, proud. He is wonderful to me. Last Christmas he gave me this diamond ring . . ."

Mrs. Norchet: "And a mink coat."

Lucille: "No, it was a stole. Christmas before it was a lamb coat. And in the spring he will get me a Pontiac convertible. Nice, eh?"

Remembering the Rocket

Lucille [on being a hockey wife]: "The worst is when he is playing on the road and I am listening on the radio and the announcer says, 'Richard is hurt, he's leaving the ice.' I almost die. He phones as soon as he can to tell me how bad it is, but it's awful waiting. It's not so bad when you see it at the Forum. When they fight with their fists, I know he's all right because he can handle himself. But when the sticks go up I get so frightened. That Howe is a dirty player, like Lach used to be."

SIDE BY SIDE: LUCILLE AND
MAURICE ON THE TOWN.

Richard
as Icon

THE ROCKET: A HERO FOR QUEBEC

by Hugh MacLennan, January 15, 1955

I DON'T THINK I'M FANCIFUL IN MY BELIEF THAT 1954 WAS A YEAR OF CHANGE IN MONTREAL.

At the moment, Canada has no real focal point, partly because we are a bilingual nation but also because the issue between Montreal and Toronto remains undecided. At stake in this inter-city rivalry is the privilege of setting the style for our growing country, and Montrealers are beginning to fear that the geographical and economic cards are stacked against them, just as they fear that the mentality of Toronto is better adjusted to the modern age than their own.

Montreal's current enthusiasm for a hockey player called Maurice Richard is probably not unconnected with the city's awareness that its prestige is being challenged. Richard has become the greatest hero Montreal has ever acknowledged,

DOUBLE BUBBLY: THE ROCKET POURS CHAMPAGNE INTO THE 1957 STANLEY CUP.

and it is obvious that his genius for hockey is only a partial cause of his apotheosis.

In many ways, Howie Morenz was a greater forward, and today Beliveau and Geoffrion are probably more useful to the team. But, as one sportswriter put it, the Rocket is terrific even while standing still. He is more interesting when he misses a goal than most men are when they connect. And when he does put the puck into the net, the Forum thunders with approval of something more than a change in the score.

It is admiration for the man himself, an identification of the city's spirit with his. For Richard is an old-fashioned personality, utterly non-conformist, relying more on élan than on cunning, with a strange courtliness even in his ferocity. There is no trace in him of the good mixer or the great guy, no pretence of being just like everyone else, no false modesty, no deliberate showmanship, no cheap appeals for popularity. He is a passionate individual.

It is to this old-fashioned individualism that Montreal responds. When Richard returned from

PHOTO BY R.H.S
SACKVILLE N.B.

IT IS ADMIRATION FOR THE MAN
HIMSELF, AN IDENTIFICATION OF

RICHARD 'HUR

Woodward To Rise Again From Ruins Of Tornado Citizens Are Determined

Half of Residents of Oklahoma City Homeless — "It Will All Come Back," Says Company Head — Known Dead 151 as Rescue Parties Search For Casualties in Panhandle Area

Woodward, Okla., April 11—(AP)—A staggered but stoical people today set about to rebuild this wind-shattered city, reduced to litter in many sections by Wednesday night's tornado which cost at least 83 lives and left approximately 2,000 of its 5,500 residents homeless.

The army flew filtering equipment into this tornado-stricken city to avert a water famine.

Oklahoma and Texas officials counted 151 dead and more than 600 injured from the storm which cut across this two-state area Wednesday night.

Mass funerals for the dead were planned for the next few days.

Grave diggers were put to work in the municipal cemetery after a special session of the city council. Afterward, Mayor R. A. Bosch announced funeral plans services probably within the next two days, depending on the weather, since no building large enough for indoor services is available.

The council decided also to condemn additional acreage adjoining the cemetery tract. The mayor said burial of the storm dead would fill up or overflow the present acreage.

Meanwhile, a group of Woodward business men and city officials planned to meet to discuss plans for rebuilding their city. Most of them felt here will be a temporary drop in population when those whose homes were demolished go elsewhere for shelter, but all have the attitude of Henry Bowman, head of a bottling company here, who said:

"WILL COME BACK"

"It will all come back. I am not in the least pessimistic, but it will take a little time."

made to restore communication and power facilities in Woodward.

This was the casualty toll as listed by the Red Cross: Woodward, 85 dead, 1,000 or more injured; Higgins, Tex., 43 dead, 232 injured; Glazier, Tex., 13 dead, 40 injured; White Horse, Okla., none dead, 30 injured; Gray County, Tex., none dead, three injured.

Property loss here was estimated at more than $3,000,000 by Alex Geismar, vice-president of a Woodward bank.

State patrolmen augmented local police forces to help guard against looting of the wind-wrecked buildings.

The storm which began its devastation at White Deer, Tex., coursed through Glazier and Higgins in Texas and then into Oklahoma. Kansas felt the backlash of the tornadic winds. Damage was inflicted on four Kansas towns, but no casualties were reported.

The state placed all available facilities at disposal of the stricken area and doctors and nurses were flown in from nearby cities and neighboring states.

IDENTIFICATION SLOW

Bodies of some of the victims were badly battered, attesting to the ferocity of the storm. Clothing was ripped from many of the dead. Identification proceeded slowly because of the disfigured bodies.

Clyde Grim, 57, of Woodward, who was injured, gave this description of the storm.

South Africa's Diamond

TELEGRAM

11. 1947   SATURDAY—Clearing, much cooler. Low tonight 33; high tomorrow 43.   **PRICE·THREE CENTS**

. WON'T PLAY

Princess

BLACK MART IN CURRENCY IS REVEALED

British Travellers In Europe Pay Heavy Fines For Getting Cash From Mystery Man

London, April 11—(CP)—Existence of a continental black market in currency, financed unwittingly by British travellers who run out of funds, was indicated today as two more persons were fined for exceeding their legal spending allowance abroad.

Sir Hamilton Westrow Hulse was fined £65 ($260), after he pleaded guilty to obtaining 24,000 francs in return for a cheque for £50.

Mrs. Mathilde Collins was fined £200 for obtaining 60,000 francs in Paris last June in return for a cheque for £100. Yesterday Mrs. Edna Clayton was fined £100 for cashing a £50 cheque at Monte Carlo last year.

All three had been issued with £35 which is the maximum sterling holiday travellers may take from Britain in one year. In each case cheques were made out to a Max Intrator now held in Paris on charges of illegal currency deals.

Intrator was not known personally to them. The defence in all three cases followed the same line: That Britons found the costs of a French holiday far more than they expected and, when their funds ran out, they were put in touch with Intrator.

F. D. Barry, who prosecuted Mrs. Collins, said the process would be for the cheques to come to London where Intrator had an account. The funds would then be transferred to the office he maintained in Cairo.

Scores of similar prosecutions are said to be pending. Scotland Yard and Treasury officials in the south of France and other popular resorts are trying to find how some British holiday-makers are able to finance

Fiery Canadien Star Tore Ligaments In Knee In Last Night's Game

"Rocket" Appears Before League President Campbell to Explain Slashing At Forum Last Night — Match Penalty Was in Order, Declares Prexy — Still Studies Case

Montreal, April 11—(CP)—Maurice (Rocket) Richard left with Montreal Canadiens for Toronto today while President Clarence Campbell of the National Hockey League considered the case of the fiery right wing star whose stick swinging against Toronto Maple Leafs last night brought him a match penalty.

Canadiens officials said Richard definitely would not play in tomorrow night's game against the Leafs, third in the best-of-seven Stanley Cup final now tied at one victory apiece. They said the Rocket tore some ligaments in his knee in the first period of last night's game when he collided with Gus Mortson of the Leafs.

Meantime, Campbell, who conferred for 40 minutes this morning with Richard after receiving referee Bill Chadwick's report of attacks Richard made on two Toronto players, said the referee's ruling in banishing the rocket for the game was correct.

Richard's match penalty came in the second period when Leafs, who won the game 4-0 were leading by three goals. The Rocket earlier had served a major penalty for flooring Rookie Vic Lynn and drawing blood and the match penalty, which carries

a $100 fine, came after he cracked Bill Ezinicki over the head.

Campbell called Richard before him this morning and the Canadien star was accompanied by Senator Donat Raymond. Club president Senator Raymond conferred again this afternoon with the league chief.

There was no indication today that Canadiens had made any move to protest the game or the penalty and it was believed such action would be unlikely, especially since Campbell has supported Chadwick's decision.

Fists Fly In Strike Row 600 Out At Weston Plant

Unknown Woman Seeks To Prove If Slayer Is Son

Non-striker Charge Picket Line — Company Rejects Union's 13½-cent Wage Demand

Chicago after scoring his four hundredth goal, he was met by a mob of enthusiasts stretching out their hands to touch him. In his honour they carried a towering *papier-maché* effigy of their hero that looked like one of those grotesque mediaeval images seen in Mardi Gras parades in the south of France. An anachronism in the middle of the 20th century?

It so happens that no hockey player has ever suffered more from illegal tactics than Maurice Richard. He is a type of player few English-speaking Canadians understand. He is that rare thing, a champion who is also an obsessed artist. Latin that he is, he might easily have been a great matador had he been born in Spain. He has the courage, the grace, the intensity, the sombre dignity. When you talk to him you feel he is as old as the hills and at the same time as young as a fresh-cheeked boy. Gentleness and ferocity both live in him. Even in a crowd he is strangely solitary. His eyes seem far away, and in hockey he has found a kind of personal destiny.

The reason he explodes is that he has again

WHEN RICHARD
RETURNED FROM
CHICAGO AFTER
SCORING HIS FOUR
HUNDREDTH GOAL,
HE WAS MET BY A
MOB OF ENTHUSI-
ASTS STRETCHING
OUT THEIR HANDS
TO TOUCH HIM.

HE IS THAT RARE THING,
A **CHAMPION** WHO IS ALSO
AN **OBSESSED ARTIST.**

and again been prevented from playing hockey as well as he can because the referees have not enforced the rules properly. Every great player must expect to be marked closely, but for ten years the Rocket has been systematically heckled by rival coaches who know intuitively that nobody can more easily be taken advantage of than a genius. Richard can stand any amount of roughness that comes naturally with the game, but after a night in which he has been cynically tripped, slashed, held, boarded and verbally insulted by lesser men he is apt to go wild. His rage is curiously impersonal — an explosion against frustration itself.

It is bad for Richard and bad for the game that this kind of emotion has grown up around him, for it spreads far beyond the hockey rinks. Richard has become more than a hero to millions of *Canadiens*. Owing to the way in which he has been (so they think) persecuted, he has imperceptibly become the focus of the persecution-anxieties latent in a minority people. Not even the fact that he is loved and admired almost

BLOODY BUT UNBOWED: RICHARD AND BRUIN SUGAR JIM HENRY AFTER HABS' WIN AGAINST BOSTON IN 1953 FINALS.

equally by English-speaking Montrealers can modify the profound self-identification of loyal *Canadiens* with this singular man.

THEY SEE IN RICHARD NOT ONLY A PERSON WHO IDEALLY EMBODIES THE FIRE AND STYLE OF THEIR RACE; THEY ALSO SEE IN HIM A MAN WHO FROM TIME TO TIME TURNS ON HIS PERSECUTORS AND ANNIHILATES THEM.

It sounds fantastic to say it, but at the moment Richard has a status with some people in Quebec not much below that of a tribal god, and I doubt if even he realizes how much of what he stands for in the public mind is only indirectly connected with the game he plays.

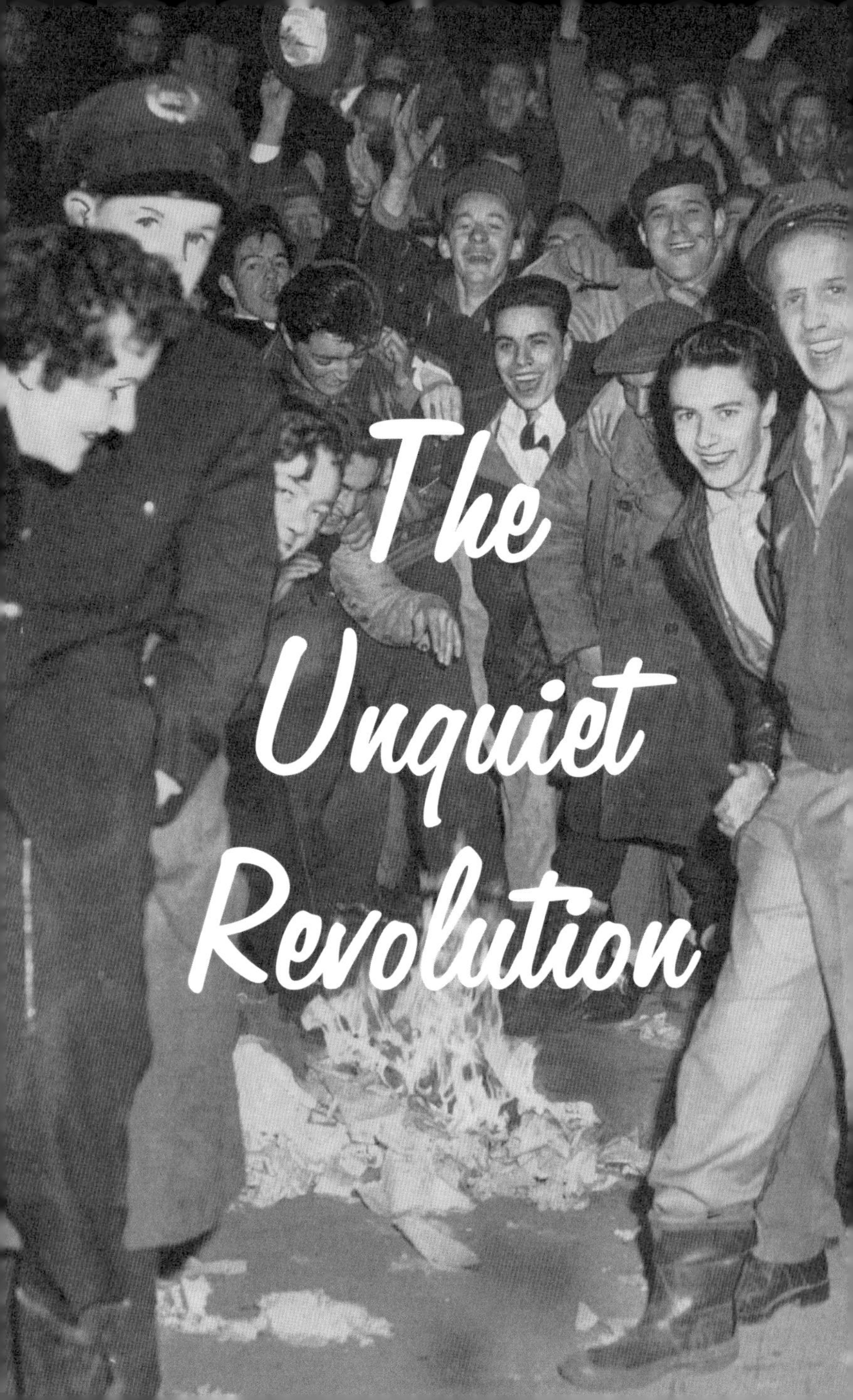
The
Unquiet
Revolution

ON MARCH 17, 1955, AT EXACTLY 9:11 P.M., A TEAR-GAS BOMB EXPLODED IN THE MONTREAL FORUM

where sixteen thousand people had gathered to watch a hockey match between the Montreal Canadiens and the Detroit Red Wings. The acrid yellowish fumes that filled the stadium sent the crowd rushing to the exits, coughing and retching. But it did more. It touched off the most destructive and frenzied riot in the history of Canadian sport.

The explosion of the bomb was the last straw in a long series of provocative incidents that swept away the last remnant of the crowd's restraint and decency. Many of the fans had come to the game in an ugly mood. The day before, Clarence Campbell, president of the National Hockey League, had banned Maurice Richard, the star of the Canadiens and the idol of the highly partisan Montreal fans, from hockey for the remainder of the season. The suspension couldn't have come at a worse time for the Canadiens. The league leadership was at stake: they were leading Detroit by the narrow margin of two points.

Richard's award for individual high scoring was at stake too – he was only two points ahead of his teammate Bernie (Boom Boom) Geoffrion. Furthermore, it had been a long tough hockey season, full of emotional outbursts. All during the first period of play the crowd had vented their anger at Campbell by shouting, "*Va t'en*, Campbell" ("Scram, Campbell") and showering him with rotten fruit, eggs, pickled pigs' feet and empty bottles. At one time there were as many as ten thousand people packed around the outside of the Forum. Many of them rushed around in bands shrieking like animals. For a time it looked as if a lynching might even be attempted: groups

BANISHED FROM THE 1955 PLAYOFFS, RICHARD WOULD HAVE HIS REVENGE, WINNING THE NEXT FIVE STANLEY CUPS.

52

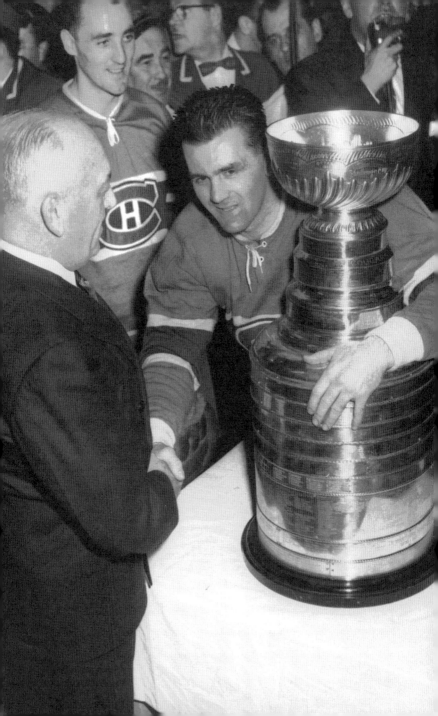

of rioters were savagely chanting in unison, "Kill Campbell! Kill Campbell!" The windows of passing streetcars were smashed and cab drivers were hauled from their vehicles and pummelled. The mob smashed hundreds of windows in the Forum. They pulled down signs and tore doors off their hinges. They toppled newsstands and telephone booths.

But the greatest damage done was not physical. Montrealers awoke ashamed and stunned after their emotional binge. The *Montreal Star* observed, "Nothing remains but shame." The *Toronto Star* commented, "It's savagery which attacks the fundamentals of civilized behaviour." A Dutch newspaper [erroneously] headlined the riot story: STADIUM WRECKED, 27 DEAD, 100 WOUNDED.

The newspapers and radio were blamed for whipping up public opinion against Campbell before the riot. Frank Hanley, of Montreal city council, said that Mayor Jean Drapeau must accept at least some of the responsibility. Had he not publicly criticized Campbell's decision to suspend Richard instead of appealing to the public to accept it? Drapeau, in turn, blamed the riot on Campbell, who "provoked it" by his presence at the game.

In the case history of the Richard riot, the night of March 13, four nights before the Montreal outburst, is important. On that night the Montreal Canadiens were playing against the Boston Bruins in the Boston Garden. An incident occurred six minutes before the end of the game which set the stage for the debacle in Montreal. Richard was skating across the Boston blueline past Boston defenceman Hal Laycoe when the latter put his stick up high and caught Richard on the left side of his head. It made a nasty gash which later required five stitches. Frank Udvari, the referee, signalled a penalty to Laycoe for highsticking but allowed the game to go on because the Canadiens had the puck.

Richard skated behind the Boston net and had returned to the blueline when the whistle blew. He rubbed his head, then suddenly skated over to Laycoe. Lifting his stick high over his

VEGETABLES, EGGS, TOMATOES, RUBBERS, BOTTLES AND PROGRAMS RAINED DOWN ON HIM. THEY WERE THROWN FROM THE $1.50 SEATS AND STANDING SECTIONS FAR ABOVE.

BUT CAMPBELL STOOD HIS GROUND.

head with both hands Richard pounded Laycoe over the face and shoulders with all his strength. Laycoe dropped his gloves and stick and motioned to Richard to come and fight with his fists. An official, linesman Cliff Thompson, grabbed Richard and took his stick away from him. Richard broke away, picked up a loose stick on the ice and again slashed away at Laycoe, this time breaking the stick on him. Again Thompson got hold of Richard, but again Richard escaped and with another stick slashed at the man who had injured him. Thompson subdued Richard for the third time by forcing him down to the ice. With the help of a teammate, Richard regained his feet and sprang at Thompson, bruising his face and blackening his eye.

Richard was penalized for the remainder of the game and fined $100. Laycoe, who suffered body bruises and face wounds, was penalized five minutes for high-sticking and was given a further 10-minute penalty for tossing a blood-stained towel at referee Udvari.

Richard's emotional and physical resistance

were at a low ebb on the night of the Boston game. It was near the end of a long exhausting schedule. The Canadiens had played Boston only the previous night in Montreal. Richard had been hurled against a net and had injured his back. He never considered sitting out the Boston game. There was too much at stake. With three scheduled games left, the Canadiens' chances of finishing first in the league were bright. Furthermore, Richard was narrowly leading the league for individual high scoring. If he won, he would receive $1,000 from the league and another $1,000 from his club.

IT'S POSSIBLE THAT RICHARD IS THE GREATEST HOCKEY PLAYER WHO EVER LIVED.

Opposing teams fully recognize Richard's talent and use rugged methods to stop him. One — and sometimes two — players are specifically detailed to nettle him. They regularly hang on to him, put hockey sticks between his legs, body-check him and board him harder than necessary. Once he skated 20 feet with two men on his shoulders to score a goal. His opponents also employ psychological warfare to unnerve him. Inspector William Minogue, who, as police officer in charge of the Forum, is regularly at rink side during games, frequently hears opposing players calling Richard "French pea soup" or "dirty French bastard" as they skate past. If these taunts result in a fight, both Richard and his provoker are sent to the penalty bench. Opposing teams consider this a good bargain.

Richard is a rarity among men as well as among hockey players. He is an artist. He is completely dedicated to playing good hockey and scoring goals. "It's the most important thing in my life," he told me.

There are better skaters, better stickhandlers,

"HIS STRENGTH COMES ALL AT ONCE LIKE THE EXPLOSION OF A BOMB" better checkers and better playmakers than Richard, but no better hockey player. He seems to have the power to summon forth all his strength at the very instant it's needed. "His strength comes all at once like the explosion of a bomb," says Kenny Reardon, an ex–hockey player who is now assistant manager of the Canadiens.

In April 1947, during a playoff game against Toronto, Richard used his stick on Vic Lynn's eye (four stitches) and on Bill Ezinicki's head (seven stitches). He was fined $250 and suspended for one game.

In March 1951, in the lobby of the Piccadilly Hotel in New York, he grabbed referee Hugh Mclean by the throat and cursed him loudly for several minutes. Richard was protesting what he considered a poor decision that was rendered at a game a few nights earlier. He was fined $500.

In December 1954 in Toronto he charged into Bob Bailey with his stick, broke two of his front teeth, then turned and struck linesman George Hayes. He was given two 10-minute misconduct penalties and fined $250.

MAURICE AND BROTHER HENRI CUT THROUGH THE BOSTON CREASE.

Three months later came the incident in Boston. Both Richard and Campbell refrained from making public statements until after the

hearing. The attacks on Laycoe and Thompson were deliberate and persistent, [Campbell] found. "An incident occurred less than three months ago in which the pattern of conduct of Richard was

MONTREAL PARTISANS SHOW WHAT
THEY THINK OF LEAGUE PRESIDENT
CLARENCE CAMPBELL.

64

almost identical . . . Consequently, the time for leniency or probation is past. Whether this type of conduct is the product of temperamental instability or wilful defiance doesn't matter. It's a type of conduct that cannot be tolerated by any player, star or otherwise." The room was completely silent as Campbell then pronounced the punishment: "Richard is suspended from playing in the remaining league and playoff games."

There were portents of what was to happen on the night of March 17 in the phone calls received by Campbell. One of the first callers said, "Tell Campbell I'm an undertaker and he'll be needing me in a few days." Another person said, "I intend to kill you and I already have a hiding place picked out."

The Montreal press, both English and French, reinforced the fans' feeling that Campbell had victimized them. *Le Matin* castigated the NHL president for penalizing the public and the fans as well as Richard. One French weekly published a crude cartoon of Campbell's head on a platter, dripping blood, with the caption: "This is how we would like to see him."

On March 17 at 11:30 a.m. came the first sign that Montreal fans would not be content to limit their protests to angry words. A dozen young men showed up at the Forum where the Canadiens were scheduled to play Detroit that night. They bore signs saying "*Vive* Richard" and "*A Bas* Campbell." The activity outside the Forum mounted steadily as the hour of the game approached. Bands of demonstrators moved up and down with signs saying "Unfair to French Canadians."

At about 6:30 a number of panel trucks circled around Atwater Park, across from the Forum, a few times and discharged a number of young men in black leather windbreakers bearing white insignia. These windbreakers had special significance for the police. They were the garb of youthful motorcyclists who had been involved in disorders on previous occasions. Other groups kept arriving steadily. By 8:30, when the game started, in addition to the Forum patrons, there were probably about six hundred demonstrators. The

"TELL CAMPBELL
I'M AN UNDERTAKER
AND HE'LL BE
NEEDING ME IN A
FEW DAYS."

Forum loudspeaker announced that all seats were now sold. A picketer shouted back, "We don't want seats. We want Campbell!" The cry was taken up and repeated endlessly with savage intensity. A few minutes after the game started Richard slipped into the Forum unnoticed and took a seat near the goal umpire's cage at the south end of the rink. He gazed intently at the ice, a look of distress on his face: the Canadiens were playing sloppy hockey. "Our players were as upset and excited as the fans," said coach Dick Irvin later. "The Richard suspension had taken the heart out of them." At the 11th minute of the first period Detroit scored a second goal and the Canadiens saw their hopes of a league championship go up in smoke. It was at this minute that Clarence Campbell entered the arena. He couldn't have chosen a worse time for his entrance.

As soon as Campbell sat down the crowd recognized him and pandemonium broke loose. They shifted their attention from the game to Campbell and set up a deafening roar. "Shoo Campbell, Shoo Campbell." The next 40 minutes were to be sheer torture for Campbell. Vegetables, eggs, tomatoes, rubbers, bottles and programs rained down on him. They were thrown from the $1.50 seats and standing sections far above.

But Campbell stood his ground. Each time he got up to remove the debris from his clothes, the clamour grew louder. Whenever the Detroit team scored the crowd's temper rose and the shower of objects on Campbell thickened. Shortly before the end of the first period, a youth in a windbreaker came down the aisle from above and told the usher he was a friend and that he wanted to shake hands with Campbell. As he approached Campbell he held out his left hand. When Campbell took his hand the youth unleashed two or three blows. Fortunately, Campbell had expected a ruse. He had grabbed his assailant's left hand firmly and leaned back as the blows fell, thus avoiding their full impact.

The first period ended. Ordinarily, Campbell spends the intermissions in the referees' room. Tonight he decided to remain in his seat, believing that this would cause less excitement.

IN RICHARD THEY SEE A HERO OF TOWERING

STRENGTH WHO SMITES DOWN HIS PERSECUTORS.

UNBEKNOWNST TO GOALTENDER GUMP
WORSLEY, AN AGITATED RICHARD TEES
OFF AGAINST NEW YORK'S IVAN IRWIN.

One André Robinson, a young man of 26 who resembles Marlon Brando, confronted Campbell. Without uttering a word he squashed two large tomatoes against Campbell's chest and rubbed them in. As he fled down the stairs Campbell kept pointing at him, signalling the two policemen to arrest him.

Now, hordes of people came rushing down from the seats far above, surrounding Campbell's box. The ill feeling against Campbell was growing more intense by the second and there was nobody to help him.

Who threw the bomb? This question has never been answered. There is no evidence that the thrower intended to befriend Campbell but that's what he may have done. Chief of Detectives George Allain later observed, "The bomb-thrower protected Campbell's life by releasing it at precisely the right moment."

The bomb landed on a wet rubber mat on the aisle adjacent to the ice surface. The people nearby didn't know what it was. Some thought that the ammonia pipes had sprung a leak; others that a fire had broken out in the basement. Within a few seconds they were coughing and choking as the fumes clogged their eyes, throats, stomachs and lungs. To protect themselves as they hurried out, they wrapped programs, handkerchiefs, scarves and coats around their faces.

Campbell was surprised when he saw the first cloud of smoke. He sniffed the air and because of his military training he immediately recognized it as tear gas. He made his way to the first-aid centre 50 feet away under the stands. Richard had also made his way to the first-aid centre but had never come face to face with Campbell because he was in a different room. He was aghast at what had happened. "This is terrible, awful," he said. "People might have been killed."

Armand Paré, head of the Montreal fire department, was unwilling to let the game continue. He felt that there was real danger of panic and fire. Campbell sent the following note to Jack Adams, the Detroit general manager: "The game has been forfeited to Detroit. You are entitled to

UNTIL
THE BOMB
EXPLODED, THE
DEMONSTRATION
OUTSIDE THE
FORUM WAS
NEITHER
DESTRUCTIVE
NOR OUT OF
CONTROL.
THE EXPLOSION,
HOWEVER,
SIGNALLED A
CHANGE OF
MOOD.

take your team on its way anytime now. Selke agrees as the fire department has ordered this building closed."

Until the bomb exploded, the demonstration outside the Forum was neither destructive nor out of control. The explosion, however, signalled a change of mood. When thousands of excited, frightened fans poured outside and joined the demonstrators it seemed to unleash an ugly mob spirit.

By 11 p.m. the crowd numbered at least ten thousand. The Forum was now virtually in a state of siege. In the 15 blocks along St. Catherine Street, east of the Forum, 50 stores were damaged and looted. By 3 a.m. the last rock had been hurled, the last window smashed and the last blood-curdling shriek of "Kill Campbell!" had been uttered. The fury of the mob had spent itself.

A View

from the

Pressbox

RATING THE ROCKET
by Andy O'Brien, Montreal Star, *November 7, 1975*

TUESDAY IS REMEMBRANCE DAY AND FORUM FANS, EVEN THOSE WITH SAD RECOLLECTIONS OF LOVED ONES WHO DIDN'T RETURN FROM OUR WARS, ARE DUE FOR AN EXCIT-ING JAUNT DOWN MEMORY LANE.

Three Canadien heroes of yesterday and today are to be honoured — the club's trio of 50-goal scorers. But watch for debates because:

Rocket Richard scored his 50 in 50 games; Boom Boom Geoffrion in 68 games; Guy Lafleur in 66 games last season.

You hear 'em stressing that the Rocket's record was set in 1944–45 when the league was weaker due to war and the Canadiens were so loaded they had five players among the six first all-stars.

Boomer buffs will argue that he scored his 50 despite missing six games due to injuries in 1960–61 when the six-team NHL was formidable.

Guy Lafleur netted no. 50 on March 29 in

only his fourth season. Some will say the league is watered down due to expansion. But I see the toughest back-checking ever; players who can't light a fire offensively are checking.

Okay, boys, let's look at career scoring averages. Up to the end of last season Lafleur's was .459 in 285 regular season games. Boomer ended with .445 in 883 games. But whoops . . . the Rocket ended with .557! He had netted 544 goals in 978 games over a span of 18 seasons that embraced peace years, war years and his own periods of truculent truce.

PERSONALLY, I RATE ROCKET THE GREATEST FORWARD OF NHL HISTORY AND I'VE SEEN THEM ALL.

Boomer likely agrees. Guy can get an idea from the greatest NHL goal ever — scored on the same Forum ice when he was a six-month infant in Thurso, Quebec.

It was the seventh and last game of a harsh semifinal playoff against Boston on April 8, 1952.

THE 50-GOAL CLUB:
RICHARD (LEFT), GUY LAFLEUR
AND BOOM BOOM GEOFFRION.

78

Score was 1–1, four minutes to go. The Rocket had been knocked out with a six-stitch head bash in the second period and returned just as coach Dick Irvin called a line change. Rocket tumbled over the boards with mates Toe Blake and Elmer Lach.

The Rocket picked up a pass from Butch Bouchard (father of Pierre) near the Canadien net, eluded a Bruin forechecker and veered toward centre-ice.

He swept around the centre's poke-check, spurted away from the other Bruin wingman, button-hooked at full speed around defenceman Bill Quackenbush, and bowled over the other defenceman, Bob Armstrong, who had tried a bodycheck as goaler Sugar Jim Henry dove. Rocket pulled away the puck and blasted it into the net. In his epic, end-to-end rush for the game-winner he had gone through or around the whole Bruin team. Later he apologized for not passing to Toe or Elmer: "My eyes were blurry."

FIREMAN RICHARD
by Dink Carroll, Montreal Gazette, *March 25, 1944*

MAURICE RICHARD IS WHAT IS KNOWN IN BASEBALL VERNACULAR AS A "FIREMAN."

He is the first guy dressed and out of the room when the game is over. After his great performance against the Leafs on Thursday, he was out of the dressing room with almost as much speed as he'd displayed in cutting around the Toronto defence earlier in the night.

He is noticeably shy and exceedingly modest, which may be the reason he is always on the lam. That "fireman" tag suits him, too; he certainly is the gent who cooled off the red-hot [Toronto Maple Leaf goalie Paul] Bibeault.

Richard is so strong physically that his teammates say he has muscles in his hair. That habit he has of going around a man on one foot and holding him off with one hand requires strength of arm and strength of leg. He doesn't speak English very well, but that hasn't anything to do with his taciturnity. Earlier in the season Dick Irvin told chatty Fernand Majeau that Richard would be his roomie on the road.

"No, no, don't do that," said Majeau. "Don't you know he never talks?"

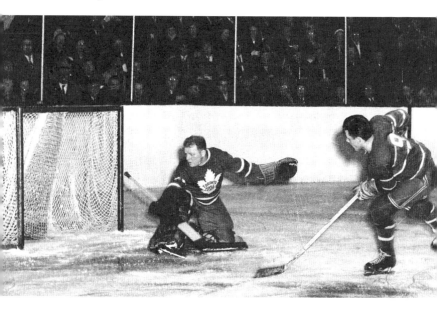

RICHARD GOES IN ON LEAF
GOALIE TURK BRODA.

Remembering the Rocket

THE RIGHT MAN FOR THE SITUATION
by Milt Dunnell, Toronto Star, *April 18, 1958*

JACQUES BEAUCHAMP, THE HOCKEY WRITER FOR A FRENCH-LANGUAGE JOURNAL, SAT CROUCHED OVER HIS PORTABLE TYPEWRITER AND ASKED ALMOST DESPAIRINGLY: "WHAT CAN YOU SAY ABOUT THE ROCKET THAT HASN'T BEEN SAID ALREADY?"

This was while the humid Montreal Forum seemed to shudder from the thunder of cheers that started deep down in the pit and rumbled up to the rafters; while the ice became littered with the debris of fanatical fans and a forlorn figure in the spangles of the Boston Bruins cut a final swath of disgust and resignation with his ponderous goal stick before disappearing into the alley leading toward the dressing room. It was while crimson-shirted sweaty men, far below the press box in the stratosphere, hugged and tugged and pummelled a fellow skater who has slick black hair, shaggy eyebrows and the most lethal shot in shinny.

Earlier, a Detroit reporter had cracked, only partly in jest: "I should ask the French-Canadian writers whether they can tell me how many play-off games Rocket Richard has won in overtime." And a partisan Boston author told a radio audience: "When a game goes into sudden-death at Montreal, the number I fear most is nine." For the benefit of any new listeners from Moscow or Mars he added the information that nine is the number worn by Le Rocket Richard, who pre-dates both Sputniks.

If it's any help to Monsieur Beauchamp now, he might say that Le Rocket Richard apparently is like all hockey men in that he has no love for overtime. So he broke up this party early. It looked as if the Habs and the Bostons might go on taking potshots at each other all night — until all hands had succumbed to exhaustion or heat prostration. Obviously, the situation called for a knockout puncher to wind up the show and get the customers home ahead of the milkman. None qualifies better than Le Rocket, who had 97 deciding goals prior to last night, according to statisticians. This one will fade gradually into the pattern of history here because Le Rocket has triggered so many big ones. But it will live in memory along with the tax on tea and Ted Williams' saliva among the things which have happened to Boston.

Actually, Le Rocket owed his employers something like this to justify whatever they pay him for an evening's work. Up to the moment when he launched that flying saucer past superman Simmons in the Boston net, Le Rocket had done remarkably little for a citizen of his stature. In fact, strangers in the house were asking the ushers whether there hadn't been some mistake in printing the program. That man with the number nine on his back definitely didn't look like the Silky Sullivan of hockey.

Some observers claimed this was only his second shot on the net. If that be true, maybe it brings up a point for less-talented artisans. Mr. Leo Labine, for example, lamented in the stillness of the Boston dressing room that the game had no business going into overtime. Leo could speak with authority since he, personally, could have sent folks home in regulation time.

Early in the first period, Leo made one of the most spectacular moves of a game that provided spectacular moves by the dozen. He intercepted a Montreal pass and scooted past Jean-Guy Talbot, one of the Montreal defenders. Leo made such a deceptive deke he practically drew the acrobatic Jacques Plante right out of his hand-knitted britches. Jacques is a famous knitter of toques and underwear, so he probably knits britches. Certainly Jacques was decoyed out of his net. Now, all that remained was for Leo to deposit the payload into the hopper. It didn't happen and Leo had no excuse.

"The puck didn't hit anything — it didn't turn on edge, it just didn't go into the net," Leo lamented. "If I'd got that goal there wouldn't have been any overtime."

History must deal with facts. There was overtime. Le Rocket accepted the puck from Dickie Moore, who had received it from Henri Richard on a faceoff. While Le Rocket manoeuvred for his shot, the Pocket Rocket skated interference in front of Simmons and Moore acted as a decoy, creating the impression that Rocket intended to give him a drop pass.

Simmons still hasn't seen that drive. If he had seen it, he probably would have grabbed it because that's what he was doing all night. No goalie ever gave away so little and lost so much. When he gave up that goal, the Stanley Cup almost surely went with it.

NO. 9 SHARES A LAUGH WITH
TOE BLAKE AND JEAN BELIVEAU.

ROCKET'S LAST DAY AS A HAB
Staff, Montreal Gazette, September 16, 1960

THE WIFE OF MAURICE (ROCKET) RICHARD SAID SHE CRIED WHEN HER FAMOUS HUSBAND TOLD HER HE HAD DECIDED TO RETIRE AFTER 18 YEARS WITH THE MONTREAL CANADIENS IN THE NATIONAL HOCKEY LEAGUE.

"Maurice had often talked to me about retirement," his wife said after the Rocket had announced his decision at a press conference in a downtown hotel. "Like everyone else I guess I didn't want to believe he was going to retire.

"When he told me he had made up his mind, it was a great shock to me. I cried. I still can't believe that I will go to Canadiens' games and not see Maurice on the ice.

"I will still go to the games to cheer Canadiens, especially my brother-in-law Henri (Pocket Rocket) Richard."

Mrs. Richard said the Rocket told 10-year-old son Normand of his decision to retire, but he kept the news from his five other youngsters in case they would spread the word among their school friends before the press conference.

Normand is the son Maurice hopes will some day wear his famous No. 9 sweater with the Canadiens.

How did Maurice spend what was possibly one of the saddest days of his career?

"Maurice went to Canadiens' practice in the morning and scored four goals and assisted on three others," said Mrs. Richard.

"When he returned home he told me he could hardly believe it was his final practice. Then for the rest of the day he hardly spoke of his plans. He had supper with the family and then mowed the lawn.

"Later he helped Normand with his home-work. About 9 o'clock he got up to leave. He kissed me and seemed deeply moved.

"I felt it, too, but I managed not to cry before he left.

"I am sure that if I had gone to the press conference with him, I would have burst out crying, and Maurice too."

LINEMATES FOREVER: HABS COACH
TOE BLAKE AND A RETIRED MAURICE
RICHARD SKATE TOGETHER AT A
CANADIENS PRACTICE

Regarding

Henri

AS A YOUNGSTER, HENRI RARELY SAW HIS FAMOUS BIG BROTHER EXCEPT ON THE ICE.

He was six when Maurice moved from the family home to marry black-haired Lucille Norchet. That left seven Richard children at home — four sons and three daughters, Henri being the second youngest child. They lived in a three-story, red-brick house on the edge of Bordeaux built by their father Onésime.

Onésime is a lean reserved man of 58 who has been building freight cars in the CPR's Angus shops near Montreal for 42 years. Old friends such as Hector Dubois, the CPR station master in

THE BROTHERS RICHARD TAKE IT TO THE NET.

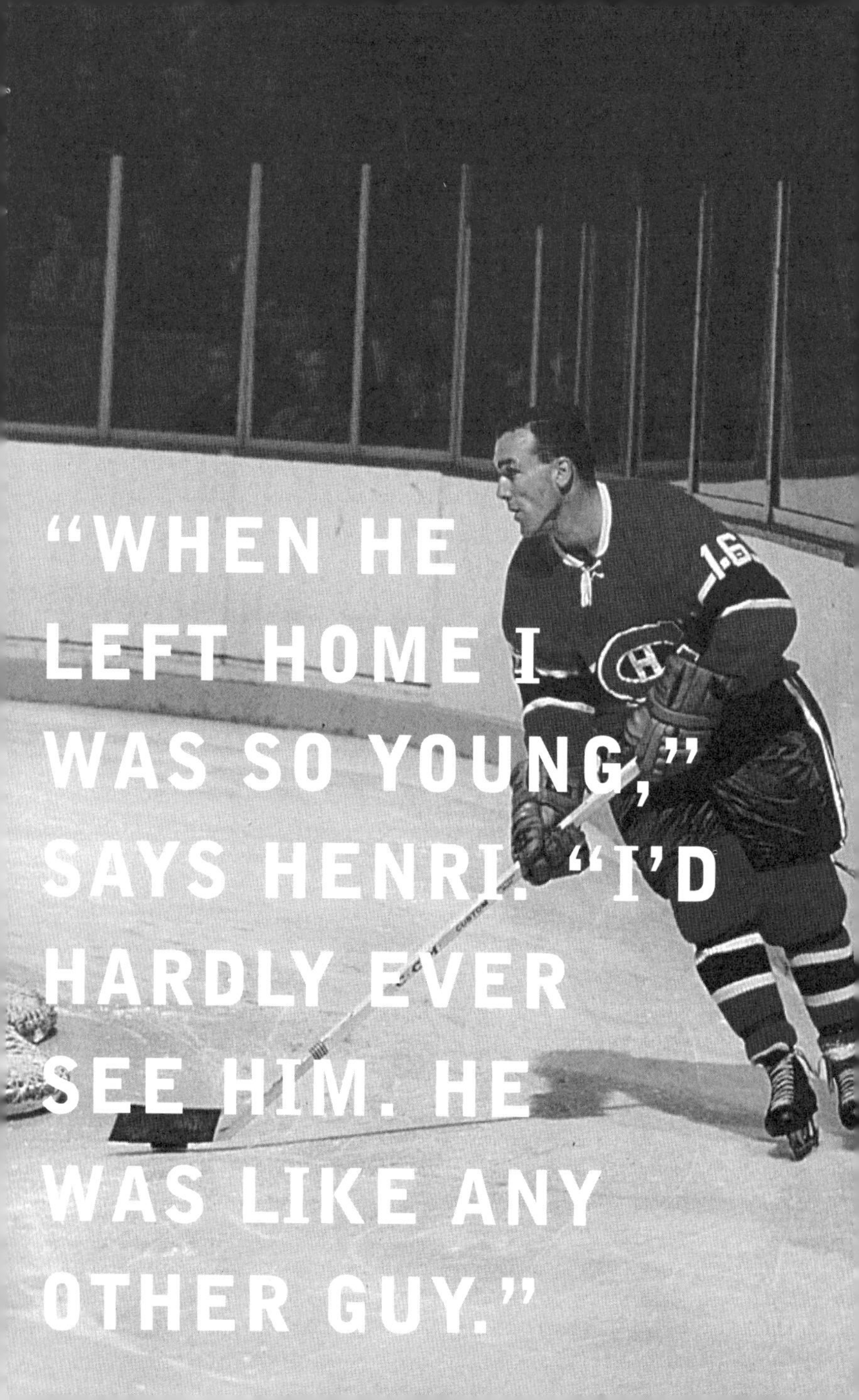

"WHEN HE LEFT HOME I WAS SO YOUNG," SAYS HENRI. "I'D HARDLY EVER SEE HIM. HE WAS LIKE ANY OTHER GUY."

the parish, say that the fierce resolution for which Maurice is renowned and with which Henri made his way to the NHL, is the heritage of Onésime.

"He is a determined worker of humble character," says Dubois. "One year after he married Alice Laramée of the parish of St. Sacrement he built his own house in partnership with his father, and became its sole proprietor without any government help or subsidies. It was remarkable at the time."

Every morning Onésime catches a train at Bordeaux to ride to the Angus shops, a small, impassive man pacing the wooden platform in front of Bordeaux's dull-red frame station. One morning, the day after young Henri had returned to the Canadiens' lineup to help beat Toronto, Guy Huot, a family friend also waiting for the train, engaged Onésime in what Huot says was a conversation typical of all those of the last 15 years.

"*Que pensez-vous de la partie d'hier?*" asked Huot. ("What do you think of the game last night?")

"*Une bonne partie,*" said Richard *père*, noncommittally.

"*Henri a fait plus que sa part*," ventured Huot. ("Henri did more than his share.")

"*Il a bien joué*," agreed Richard shortly.

At this point, says Huot, the train arrives to end the conversation, or the train does not arrive and the conversation ends.

During Canadien games at the Forum, Richard *père* is similarly unmoved. He stares solemnly at the game and the only time he shows emotion is if one of the boys scores a goal. Then, with a quick movement of his clenched right fist, like a fighter delivering a sharp hook, he'll cry out "Maurice!" if it's the Rocket who has scored, or "Henri!" and then return to his stolid vigilance.

Family friends say that all eight of the Richard children have this reserve, and Madame Richard, too, is a quiet woman, built along the comfortable lines of television's Madame Plouffe. Toe Blake, the Canadien coach, tells of a time when an American reporter, desirous of inter-viewing Henri, asked if the young player spoke English.

"I'm not sure that he even speaks French,"

"OH, MAURICE,"
HE SAID, SAVOURING
THE NAME. "NOBODY
ELSE COULD SCORE A
GOAL LIKE HIM."

Blake smiled. "He just doesn't speak."

Maurice and Henri rarely exchange a word in the Canadien dressing room and if they do it's perfunctory. Maurice never gives Henri advice, and never has. And Henri is so constituted that he never asks for it, and never has. Guy Huot, the family friend in Bordeaux, explains it.

"You know, those guy, they won't give — how you say it? — *conseil*?" he says.

"Counsel?" it was suggested.

"*Oui*, counsel — ah — instruction," he adds emphatically. "Those guy in that family never give it. And Henri doesn't want it. He wants to make his own way. He is relentless."

Henri is unstinting in his praise of his brother — "No one ever will do as well as he has done" — yet theirs is not the usual brotherly relationship. "When he left home I was so young," says Henri. "I'd hardly ever see him. He was like any other guy."

It may be significant that when Henri's parents took him to the Forum to watch the Canadiens he did not have eyes for the Rocket.

When he was asked what seemed to be a ridiculous question, "Who was your favourite player?" Henri replied, "Ted Kennedy and Elmer Lach, and Red Kelly, too."

"Why?"

"Well, Kennedy and Lach would always get the faceoffs. And they would work like hell, too."

"And Kelly?"

"He would skate so well, and play defence and forward both."

"What about Gordie Howe?"

"He seemed kind of lazy," said Henri.

And then, he added quickly, "But of course he is very good."

"And what about Maurice?"

"Oh, Maurice," he said, savouring the name. "Nobody else could score a goal like him."

Rocket in Repose

AT HOME WITH "THE MAURICE RICHARDS"

by June Callwood, May 9, 1959

MAURICE RICHARD AND HIS WIFE LUCILLE LIVE WITH THEIR SEVEN CHILDREN IN A 13-ROOM STONE HOUSE ON THE NORTHEAST SHORE OF THE ISLAND ON WHICH MONTREAL IS BUILT.

Their living room windows overlook a strip of park beyond which is the river where in summer the Richard boat is in constant use, towing the older children or their father on water skis.

Some of the appointments inside the Richard home could be transposed, just as they are, to a Maurice Richard wing on hockey's hall of fame. The wrought-iron frame of the mirror, in the front hall, for instance, is studded with four-hundreth-, five-hundreth- and six-hundreth-goal pucks. Lucille has stored literally dozens of cups, statues

MAURICE, LUCILLE AND THREE
OF THEIR BROOD POSE WITH
DAD'S TROPHIES.

and plaques in a glass-doored case in the recreation room.

Lucille Richard is a small, animated, pretty woman with mildly red hair and blue eyes. Guilelessly gay and friendly, she is also a severely clean housekeeper who keeps even the plastic flowers on the coffee table dust-free.

She possesses a kind of scented femininity that seems faintly other world, having a cigarette or drink only rarely, and wearing slacks not at all. Only daughter of Mr. and Mrs. Lucien Norchet, the former a butcher of comfortable means, Lucille was raised in a warm, hearty household that was a gathering place for her friends and any number of people her two older brothers might happen to bring home, including, one day, Richard, who was then a 17-year-old junior scoring sensation on a local team.

When Lucille first met Maurice he was attending technical school, taking training as a machinist. Hockey was a hobby; he never considered it as a career. When she was 17 and he was well into his 20th year, Maurice proposed and

Lucille accepted. Neither had ever dated anyone else. The Norchets approved of young Richard but were appalled at the couple's youth. Despite the objections, Lucille and Maurice were married the following year.

It was 1942 and Maurice was earning $40 dollars a week as a machinist in the CPR shops, making extra money in the winter playing for the Canadien Seniors. Neither spoke a word of English and when Maurice began to play for the NHL Canadiens the following winter, Lucille drank coffee with the players' wives before the games and was taught English. "I was the youngest wife and Mrs. Toe Blake and Mrs. Kenny Mosdell were so kind to me." Maurice was learning from the players and from watching movies in the strange cities where the team travelled to play. He was wretched with loneliness, developing the protective veneer of cold hostility that he outgrew only recently.

A thick-bodied, not tall, man, Richard normally has an expression of remote sadness and his black eyes are fathomless. "It will be very

"WE DON'T TALK MUCH,
JUST GET READY AND DRIVE
DOWN TO THE FORUM."

hard on me when I quit hockey," he says, seated on the living room chesterfield. He attributes his love of hockey to "the big thrill before and after every game. Before, you keep wanting the game to start, but you're afraid, too. You're afraid of a bad injury, or not playing a good game. That's what I think about all day of a game. Then, when you start to play and begin to sweat, it all goes away and you feel good."

The day of a game, Lucille tries to keep the children in the recreation room so the house will be quieter. Maurice goes to a players' meeting in the morning, returns and at three o'clock has a filet mignon, medium, one potato, a vegetable, some tomato juice, maybe fruit or ice cream. "For 16 years I have been fixing the same food, 16 years," Lucille murmurs in gathering astonishment. "*Sixteen years!* Then Maurice lies down to sleep but he doesn't sleep — just lies there. He comes out of the room around five or six. I say, 'Did you sleep?' and he says 'No.' We don't talk much, just get ready and drive down to the Forum."

Lucille is reflective: "I don't know what we will do when there is no more hockey. The first year is going to be terrible, just terrible for him." Even as an active player, Richard concedes that he's never been completely satisfied with his performance. "If I get three, four goals, I know some of them have been lucky ones. You can't be proud of yourself for that."

The subject of Richard's fame reveals ambivalence in both partners. Lucille mourns, "We can't go anywhere, can't eat in a restaurant, can't walk down the street but somebody comes over to talk to Maurice. And he must smile and be pleasant, while his dinner gets cold." Says Maurice: "Sometimes I get fed up, but I can't let it show. I don't believe it when people make a fuss over me. When it is all over, I'll be a guy like anyone else."

Richard's modesty extends to his candid self-appraisal in relation to other NHL stars. "Howe is better than me, [Milt] Schmidt was better. Elmer Lach, lots of guys are better than me. Beliveau, Geoffrion, lots of guys on the [1959] Canadiens are better hockey players than me." Richard has a

TOP: MAURICE WITH HIS FAMILY
ON THE ICE. BOTTOM: MAURICE
WITH HIS ON-ICE FAMILY.

106

one-word answer as to why he's such a force on the ice: "Desire."

Applause is small solace for Richard when he isn't scoring at his usual pace. Depression sets in, clinging to him till the scoring drought abates. "That's true, I feel terrible. I keep away from people and when the Forum is empty I go there by myself and skate. I practise shooting at the net, shooting, shooting, trying to loosen up."

Of his pre-game ritual of making the sign of the cross, he shrugs, "I always do that, ever since I started to play hockey. It's a habit. I'm a Catholic, that's all. I'm a fair Catholic, not a real good one."

Family is obviously important to Richard — he softens noticeably in the presence of his children — but he has a difficult time articulating his views on domestic harmony. "A husband and wife should not have . . ." he falters. Trying again, he says, "They must have different . . . characters." He isn't happy with the word but it will have to do. "Also," he adds, "the woman should not be the boss. That's the worst thing."

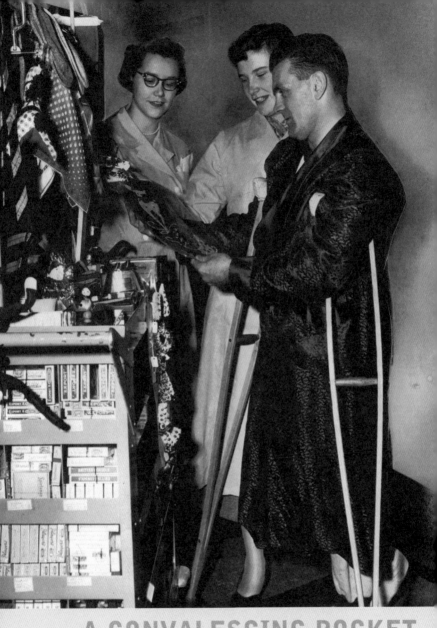

A CONVALESCING ROCKET
CHARMS TWO OF HIS FANS.

Of his children, he says, "They can have any-thing they want, anything at all. I want them home or else I want to know where they are and who they are with. That's the only rule. Rocket [junior] was going to a school where he hung around afterwards with the rest of the boys. I took him out and put him in another school. Now he comes home. And [eldest daughter] Hugette, she goes skiing on the weekends and the priest is always with them. If the children are at home or with good people, they are not getting into trou-ble, that's for sure."

His sense of family extends to his teammates. "We get along good. On road trips we all eat together, go to movies together. There's never an argument among our players. Some other teams have players who argue with one another even during a game. Not us, we are friends."

Later, Richard continues his conversation in the stands of the empty Montreal Forum, where arena staff are preparing for an evening wrestling bout. During a lunch-hour break in the workers' routines, Richard stares at the ice, where his hunched figure, skating raggedly with wounded-animal fury, has scored hundreds of goals. A sense of old ghosts makes him speak heavily, slowly and sadly.

"I've thought about nothing but hockey all my life. There's a lot I've missed. I don't read books, only magazines on the train. Lots of times I am ashamed because people are talking about things I never heard about.

"Every year I think I ought to get interested in another business, start a restaurant or something. But when the hockey starts I forget about anything else. Maybe if I had other interests, I wouldn't have lasted so long in hockey."

He confesses to fears: "I am afraid of the future. I am afraid to grow older. I never used to think of it, now it's on my mind every day. I will be so lonely when hockey is over for me."

He admits, too, that his nerves have always made it hard to get a good night's rest. "My stomach nerves were very bad for a while. I don't sleep, maybe four or five hours a night. The rest of the time I lie awake. I don't know why."

The workmen return and the lights come on with splintering brightness. They look at the man in the dark overcoat, look away, look again. Richard doesn't see them.

"I've heard other hockey players say that this is their last season, that they think they will retire at the end of the year. I don't know how they can say it. I couldn't make myself say that. I love hockey so much. I couldn't say such a thing.

"When I was young I used to skate for nothing. Now I save it for a burst when I think I can score. I have to do it that way."

The brightness of the rink and the curiosity of the workmen suddenly embarrass him. He rises to leave. In the lobby, people lined up before ticket windows see him and nudge one another in excitement.

"I've got a little put by," Richard was saying, "but not enough to live on for the rest of my life. I'll have to work. But what can I do? I don't know anything but hockey." He shrugs, turns and limps away.

The Lion in Winter

"I STILL THINK ABOUT IT TODAY," ROCKET RICHARD ADMITS.

"I still have a grudge. I still don't know if it was (Clarence) Campbell who did it, or if it was the owners of the five other teams who didn't want me in the playoffs."

No one who grew up in the province of Quebec has to ask what "it" is. No one who followed the comet that was the career of Maurice Richard would be surprised to hear that Campbell's decision to suspend Richard from the 1955 playoffs still bothers the Rocket today.

"I agreed with the suspension. I knew I would be suspended the last three games of the season. He could have suspended me for 10 or 15 games the following year. But not the playoffs."

For decades, Richard would not say whether he knew he was punching a linesman when he turned on Cliff Thompson during that infamous game in Boston and hit him twice in the face.

"I knew who it was," [Richard says now, 41 years after the incident.] "I told him three times to let go. No one was holding (Hal) Laycoe. He was punching me."

When Richard missed the last three games of that season, teammate Boom Boom Geoffrion passed him to win the scoring title by a single point. That was one title that would escape Richard in his career; for outscoring the Rocket, Geoffrion received death threats from Montreal fans.

* * *

With the Montreal Forum down to its last two hockey games, [Richard is] in demand for interviews, public appearances, autographs. "It's too much," he says. "Too much."

There is nothing new in his reticence; he has never liked interviews and he especially dislikes the TV camera. Richard [can be] blunt and open, but that doesn't mean he likes to talk; he never did.

RICHARD INSISTS THAT THE
END OF THE LINE FOR THE OLD
FORUM, THE SCENE OF SO
MANY OF HIS TRIUMPHS,
DOESN'T AFFECT HIM AND THAT
HE IS PERFECTLY CONTENT TO
SEE THE TEAM MOVE ON TO
THE MOLSON CENTRE.

"Elmer Lach (Richard's long-time centre) rode him for years," says [another former teammate] Dickie Moore. "Rocket never said a word. He just took it and took it and took it. I think there was just one time after maybe seven years when he got up enough nerve to suggest that Elmer might have hit him with a pass just a bit sooner."

"Even when he was the captain," says Beliveau, "he didn't say much. He didn't have to. He would just look at you with those eyes."

Richard insists that the end of the line for the old Forum, the scene of so many of his triumphs, doesn't affect him and that he is perfectly content to see the team move on to the Molson Centre. "It doesn't bother me. The only thing that makes me mad is that people who love hockey will have to pay so much more

money to see the game."

Like many players of his era, the Rocket will never feel comfortable with the money aspect of today's game. Richard once [remarked] that players in his day were "virtual slaves." Today he qualifies that remark. "I mean that we were slaves in the way we were paid," he says, "not the way we were treated on the ice.

"I never made more than $50,000 in one season, and that's counting bonuses and Stanley Cup money."

When he retired in 1960, the Canadiens gave Richard a low-level public relations job. Richard wanted a voice in the hockey operations; he especially wanted to work to develop young players. The Canadiens wanted him to be a glorified handshaker. For four years he bit his tongue and bore the humiliation in silence.

"I had two things to do in my office," Richard wrote in his weekly column in *Dimanche Matin* after he quit. "I opened the blinds at 9 and I closed them at 5."

Maurice and Lucille Richard still had children

RICHARD SAYS HE NEVER MADE MORE THAN $50,000 A SEASON – "AND THAT'S COUNTING BONUSES AND STANLEY CUP MONEY."

to feed and clothe, so Richard did what he could to support his family. He opened his No. 9 tavern — and closed it three years later. He took a job as an ordinary salesman with S. Albert & Co., a supplier of home heating oil. He made house calls, the most ferocious scorer in the history of the National Hockey League sitting down with the head of the household to discuss a fuel-oil purchase. Eventually he became a vice-president at S. Albert, which to this day uses his name and title in its ad in the yellow pages.

In 1967, Richard started his own company, General Fishing Lines. He imported fishing line from the U.S., had it wound onto plastic spools by his one woman employee, then meticulously hand-labelled the spools and shipped them all over Canada himself.

In 1972, Richard became the first coach of the Quebec Nordiques in the World Hockey Association. He lasted 15 days. Stories at the time suggested he couldn't take the pressure; Richard says he couldn't stand being away from his family in Montreal.

MAURICE VO: The change was so gradual ...

no one even noticed.

COACH OC: Hey, Richard! Two minutes for looking so good!

After he left the Canadiens, the rift with Molson and the Canadiens was so deep that when Richard made public appearances, it was always for Dow, O'Keefe or Labatt. For years, he refused

even to drink Molson beer. He stuck with the fuel-oil and fishing-line business and, when his hair began to turn grey, did commercials for Grecian Formula hair dye ["Hey Richard! Two minutes for looking so good!"]

Richard resolutely stayed away from ceremonies at the Forum to honour Blake and Beliveau, but when younger brother Henri was given a night on January 26, 1974, Irving Grundman persuaded the Rocket to take part.

Richard did not officially rejoin the organization until he agreed in July 1980 to represent the club at public events. Unfortunately, he was never

MAURICE AND LUCILLE.

given the opportunity to have any input into the Canadiens' operation. Richard begged Sam Pollock, Claude Ruel and Ron Caron to draft Mike Bossy in 1977 — but the club ignored him and took Mark Napier with the 10th pick.

The Rocket still keeps up a busy schedule between personal appearances and refereeing old-timers' games. He has fished and hunted all his life and that is where he is happiest today. "It's quiet there," he says simply. "There's no one to bother you."

Lucille, Richard's wife of 51 years, died in July 1994. In part to escape his grief, Richard kept up a gruelling schedule refereeing games on the old-timers' circuit that winter, officiating 55 games in all and 29 in a 30-day stretch, a brutal pace for a man of any age.

***

After Richard announced his retirement, a reporter asked [coach Toe] Blake how he would replace the Rocket.

"With two men," Blake growled.

MAURICE RICHARD 9

REGULAR SEASON

YEAR	TEAM	GP	G	A	PTS	PIM
1942-43	Mtl.	16	5	6	11	4
1943-44	Mtl.	46	32	22	54	45
1944-45	Mtl.	50	50	23	73	46
1945-46	Mtl.	50	27	21	48	50
1946-47	Mtl.	60	45	26	71	69
1947-48	Mtl.	53	28	25	53	89
1948-49	Mtl.	59	20	18	38	110
1949-50	Mtl.	70	43	22	65	11
1950-51	Mtl.	65	42	24	66	97
1951-52	Mtl.	48	27	17	44	44
1952-53	Mtl.	70	28	33	61	112
1953-54	Mtl.	70	37	30	67	112
1954-55	Mtl.	67	38	36	74	125
1955-56	Mtl.	70	38	33	71	89
1956-57	Mtl.	63	33	29	62	74
1957-58	Mtl.	28	15	19	34	28
1958-59	Mtl.	42	17	21	38	27
1959-60	Mtl.	51	19	16	35	50
TOTALS		978	544	421	965	1285
PLAYOFF TOTALS		133	82	44	126	188

NHL CAREER HIGHLIGHTS

WON THE STANLEY CUP IN 1943-44, 1945-46, 1952-53, 1955-56, 1956-57, 1957-58, 1958-59, 1959-60

WON THE PRINCE OF WALES TROPHY (1st place regular season) IN 1943-44, 1944-45, 1945-46, 1946-47, 1955-56, 1957-58, 1958-59, 1959-60

WON THE HART TROPHY IN 1946-47

8-TIME MEMBER OF THE FIRST ALL-STAR TEAM

6-TIME MEMBER OF THE SECOND ALL-STAR TEAM

FIRST PLAYER TO SCORE 50 GOALS IN 50 GAMES (1944-45)

MOST OVERTIME GOALS IN PLAYOFFS (6)

MOST CAREER GOALS IN STANLEY CUP FINALS (34)

MOST CAREER OVERTIME GOALS IN STANLEY CUP FINALS (3)

MOST YEARS IN STANLEY CUP FINALS (12)

TIED WITH DETROIT'S TED LINDSAY FOR MOST GOALS IN ONE PLAYOFF GAME (4)

APPOINTED ASSISTANT CAPTAIN IN 1952 AND CAPTAIN IN 1956

MEMBER OF THE FAMOUS PUNCH LINE WITH ELMER LACH AT CENTRE AND TOE BLAKE AT LEFT WING

INDUCTED INTO THE HOCKEY HALL OF FAME, JUNE 1961

Grateful acknowledgement is made for permission to reprint newspaper and magazine articles in this book:

CALLWOOD, JUNE. "The Maurice Richards." *Maclean's.* May 9, 1959. (Adapted by permission.) **CARROLL, DINK.** "Fireman Richard." Montreal *Gazette.* March 25, 1944. **DUNNELL, MILT.** "The Right Man for the Situation." *Toronto Star.* April 18, 1958. **FRAYNE, TRENT.** "Hockey's Greatest Scoring Machine." *Maclean's.* November 1, 1951. **FRAYNE, TRENT.** "How the 'Pocket Rocket' Beat His Kid-Brother Jinx." *Maclean's.* March 29, 1958. **KATZ, SIDNEY.** "The Strange Forces Behind the Richard Hockey Riot." *Maclean's.* September 17, 1955. **MacLENNAN, HUGH.** "Letter From Montreal." *Saturday Night.* January 15, 1955. Reprinted with permission of the Hugh MacLennan Estate. **O'BRIEN, ANDY.** "Rocket Greatest." *Montreal Star.* November 7, 1975. **TODD, JACK.** "The Lion in Winter." Montreal *Gazette.* March 9, 1996. "'Still Can't Believe It' the Rocket's Wife Says." Montreal *Gazette.* September 16, 1960.

Grateful acknowledgement is made for use of photographs to the following: Montreal *Gazette* (photos on pages ii, vi, viii, 2, 4, 5, 7 (bottom), 8, 9, 10 (all), 13, 14, 16, 19, 20 (all), 28, 30, 32, 34, 36, 38, 41, 45 (all), 48, 50, 53, 54, 58, 61, 62, 64, 67, 70, 76, 79, 84, 91, 92, 100, 104, 107 (all), 109, 112, 114, 117 (all), 118, 119, 121, 124, jacket (back)); Michael Leonetti Sports Products Inc. (photos on pages 24, 88, 94, 97, jacket (front)); Imperial Oil — Turofsky/Hockey Hall of Fame (photos on pages 7 (top), 26, 82); Graphic Artists/Hockey Hall of Fame (photo on page 6); York University Archives (photo on page 42); Combe Inc. Canada (photos on page 123); and *La Presse* (photo on page 46).

Every effort has been made to secure permissions to reprint material reproduced in this book. The editor and publisher will gladly receive information that will enable them to rectify in subsequent editions of this book any inadvertent errors or omissions.